THEN & NOW

HAMTRAMCK

OPPOSITE: Born of heavy industry, modern Hamtramck was a city of steel and smoke for decades. Until 1910, Hamtramck was a sleepy farming village. But the establishment of factories like Dodge Main, which forms the backdrop of this scene, changed the character of the town, burying the fields under bricks and steel. The area of Denton and Miller Streets on the South End typified the industrial landscape— gritty and hard yet teeming with life and character. (Courtesy of the Hamtramck Historical Commission.)

THEN & NOW

HAMTRAMCK

Greg Kowalski

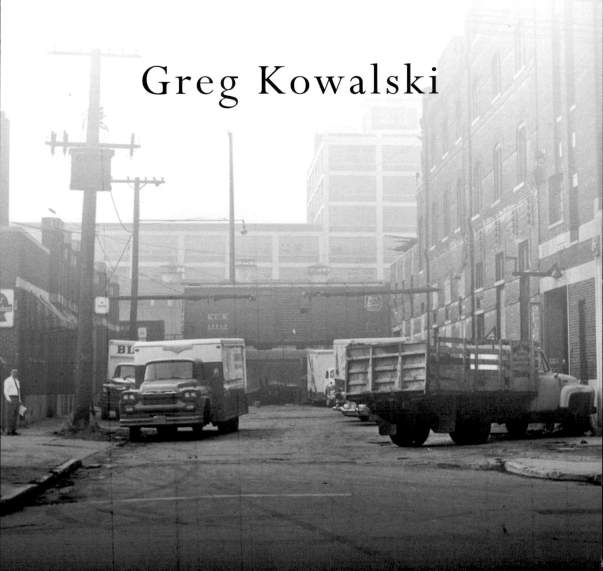

ON THE FRONT COVER: In 1962, Col. John Francis Hamtramck came home. Colonel Hamtramck died in 1803 and was buried for many years at Mount Elliott Cemetery in Detroit before being moved to Veterans Memorial Park in Hamtramck and reinterred in front of the veterans' monument. Memorial Day ceremonies are still held at the grave. (Courtesy of the Hamtramck Historical Commission.)

ON THE BACK COVER: City councilman John Wojtylo cuts a fine figure of a dapper gentleman farmer as he promotes the value of planting victory gardens during World War II. Such gardens were common in Hamtramck. In the 1960s, this site at Carpenter and Dequindre Streets became the route of the I-75 freeway. (Courtesy of the Hamtramck Historical Commission.)

Copyright © 2010 by Greg Kowalski
ISBN 978-0-7385-7735-7

Library of Congress Control Number: 2009933634

Published by Arcadia Publishing
Charleston SC, Chicago IL, Portsmouth NH, San Francisco CA

Printed in the United States of America

For all general information contact Arcadia Publishing at:
Telephone 843-853-2070
Fax 843-853-0044
E-mail sales@arcadiapublishing.com
For customer service and orders:
Toll-Free 1-888-313-2665

Visit us on the Internet at www.arcadiapublishing.com

CONTENTS

Acknowledgments

All the material in this book came from the archives of the Hamtramck Historical Commission, for which I am grateful. I would also like to thank my mother, Martha Violet Kowalski, who has always been my greatest supporter, and Joanne Sobczak for being there.

INTRODUCTION

A city is a living thing. It is born, it grows, and it can even die. It develops its own personality made up of thousands or even millions of stories. For above all else, a city is a story of people—they are what gives it life. In that respect, Hamtramck, Michigan, is typical, but its story is unique in so many other ways that it stands alone. Founded in 1798 as a township, Hamtramck was named after a French Canadian, Jean Francois Hamtramck, who legally changed his name to John Francis Hamtramck when he came to America to fight the British as a soldier in the Continental Army.

For the first 112 years of its existence, Hamtramck was a rural community mainly inhabited by German farmers. In 1901, a 2.1-square-mile portion of the township split off to form the village of Hamtramck. What remained of Hamtramck Township was absorbed piece by piece by the city of Detroit, which eventually completely surrounded Hamtramck, leaving it a little independent island.

The village of Hamtramck incorporated as a city in 1922, but the story of modern Hamtramck dates to 1910, when brothers John and Horace Dodge decided to build an automobile factory at the southeast corner of the village near some railroad lines. Shortly after construction of the plant began, the call went out for workers, and the response was staggering. From a population of about 3,500 people in 1910, Hamtramck exploded to embrace 48,000 residents by 1920. That number would climb to 56,000 by 1930. Almost all of the new residents were Polish immigrants who came to the town to work in the Dodge factory, which in time came to be known affectionately as Dodge Main.

By the time Hamtramck incorporated as a city in 1922, it had taken its place as one of the largest cities in Michigan and was becoming a national industrial powerhouse. Dodge Main, spanning 5 million square feet of floor space on 135 acres of land, came to define Hamtramck. In the process, it helped transform Hamtramck as pastures were plowed under to be replaced by paved streets flanked by factories, homes, churches, and stores. Eighty-five percent of the houses in Hamtramck were built between 1915 and 1930, and most of the stores along Jos. Campau, the main shopping district, opened in the 1920s.

Jos. Campau quickly grew to be the second most popular shopping district in southeast Michigan, ranking only behind Detroit. Along with stores, it housed restaurants, bars, and nightspots, including the Bowery Nite Club, which became one of the most popular clubs in the Midwest, attracting top acts like Sophie Tucker, the Three Stooges, and Jimmy Durante. Today all that remains of the Bowery is the ghostly image of where it once stood, imprinted on the adjoining building.

Hamtramck has changed greatly over the years. The earliest wood buildings that once lined Jos. Campau are long gone, as are other early structures like the original Immaculate Conception Ukrainian Catholic Church, which was replaced at the dawn of World War II by an impressive stone structure. Dodge Main is also gone, virtually without a trace. In 1981, it was demolished, with even the underground footings uprooted to make room for the General Motors Detroit-Hamtramck assembly plant.

Amazingly, much of the past not only still stands, but is thriving. Holbrook Elementary School was built in 1898 and remains in use, perhaps as the longest functioning school in the state. The quaint fireplaces and built-in bookshelves still can be found in some rooms. Likewise, Hamtramck High School, which opened in 1931 as Copernicus Junior High School, is still in use and has changed relatively little over the years. Copernicus was one of the most modern schools in America, and it serves as a reminder of Hamtramck's important contributions to education. The school district's 1927 school code was so progressive that it influenced school districts nationwide.

St. Francis Hospital was built in 1927 to serve the growing immigrant population and was originally known as Hamtramck Municipal Hospital. It closed in 1969 and reopened shortly after that to be used as Hamtramck City Hall. Although the building has been extensively remodeled, it still sports its original exterior features and charming interior elements, like the laundry chute in the main hallway.

Institutions still show strong reflections of the past. St. Florian Catholic Church opened in 1928 with a crowd of several thousand attending the dedication. People standing on its massive front stairs today will see almost exactly what the crowd saw on that day in October 1928. The magnificent, modified English Gothic building stands virtually frozen in time.

And there are many more examples, mostly overlooked; their significance often long forgotten. There' is a certain comfort in the stability of historic things. They stir nostalgic memories as they impart a sense of history. They also help define a town, reflecting its character and preserving what it once was as it contrasts what it has become. The lasting landmarks of Hamtramck stand as proud reminders of the city's rich history. Take a look.

CHAPTER 1

BUILDING A CITY

St. Anne's Community House, in many ways, was a counterpart of the Tau Beta Community House, which helped immigrants blend into American society. St. Anne's was founded in 1921 at 2441 Andrus Street. It provided a variety of services, including English lessons and naturalization classes, as well as playing host to numerous clubs. It helped build Hamtramck into a modern American town, although inhabited primarily by Polish immigrants. Today the house is a private residence. (Photograph courtesy of the Bentley Historical Library, University of Michigan.)

In 1798, Hamtramck was formed as a township that stretched from the Detroit River to Base Line (Eight Mile Road), and from Woodward Avenue through the Grosse Pointes. Almost immediately, the growing city of Detroit began to annex portions of the township. In 1901, a 2.1-square-mile section of the township split off and formed the village of Hamtramck. The village incorporated as a city in 1922, which is reflected in the shaded area.

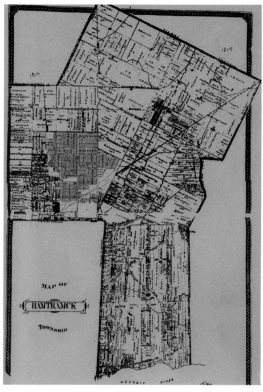

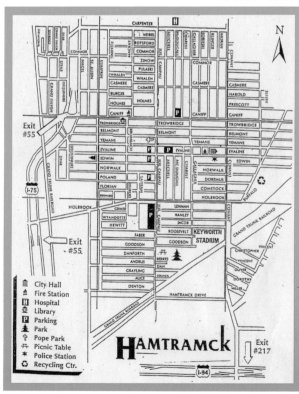

The Dickinson farmhouse was a typical example of Hamtramck's preindustrial days. The farm, between Edwin and Norwalk Streets near Gallagher, was donated to the city's school system and became the site of Dickinson School, which was built in 1913 with an initial class of 260 pupils. It burned in 1916, was rebuilt the following year, and was extensively remodeled in later years. Dickinson continues to serve as an active school.

Dodge Bros. Automobile Plant, Detroit, Mich.

Nothing had a greater influence on the development of Hamtramck than Dodge Main. Construction started in 1910 and continued almost until the factory closed in 1979. It was the magnet that drew the Polish immigrants to Hamtramck. At its peak during World War II, Dodge Main employed more than 45,000 people and covered 5 million square feet of floor space. It ultimately would be replaced by another great factory, the 3-million square-foot General Motors Detroit-Hamtramck assembly plant. That plant's massive powerhouse now occupies the site where Dodge Main was located.

Hamtramck became an often uncomfortable mix of heavy industry and homes once the Dodge Main factory opened in 1910. But Dodge Main was not the only factory in town. Chevrolet Gear and Axle was founded in 1917, straddling Hamtramck's southwestern border with Detroit. It remains clearly visible from homes on Lumpkin Street, the next block over. Now it is the American Axle plant, and the cross street has been absorbed by the Metropolitan Baking Company.

Holbrook Avenue divided the Chevrolet Gear and Axle plant complex in the earliest days and continues to do so today, although the business is now known as American Axle. Over the years, the street was widened, and the railroad tower that stood next to the tracks has been removed. The factory buildings also have been given a layer of siding that, while covering the rows of windows, has given the buildings a trim, modern, and clean look.

By 1923, there were 23 factories spewing smoke in Hamtramck, mainly as suppliers of the Dodge Main plant. They were embedded in the residential neighborhoods, often on the same blocks as houses. The Ida window and door factory, with its distinctive water tower, loomed over Dan Street for years. The lot alongside it is still empty, but modern technology prevails, with a cellular telephone tower now dominating the view.

Tau Beta was critical in shaping modern Hamtramck. It arrived in 1914 and provided many services, including legal and medical aid, as well as recreational activities. The big community house on Hanley Street was built in 1928. When Tau Beta left Hamtramck in 1958, the building was converted into Immaculate Conception Ukrainian Catholic High School. It later fell into disrepair, but in recent years, it has been extensively renovated and now houses the Hanley International Academy charter school.

Hamtramck Municipal Hospital was built in 1927. In 1931, the city leased it to the Sisters of St. Francis, who renamed it St. Francis Hospital. One of the most storied buildings in Hamtramck, the hospital closed in 1969 but soon reopened as Hamtramck City Hall on a temporary basis. It still is city hall and was remodeled and modernized in recent years. Many Hamtramckans were born in the hospital, which has been recognized as a historic site by the State of Michigan.

The Gray Ladies served in a variety of ways as volunteer assistants at St. Francis Hospital to the regular staff. Through the years, the Gray Ladies held many membership drives to recruit volunteers. Such was the case in October 1953, when Pauline Schmidt (left) signed up to be a Gray Lady and serve with Emily Lewandowski (center) and Irene Banaszwiewicz. Today the only sign of the Gray Ladies in St. Francis Hospital is a uniform on display in the main hallway of the building, which now serves as Hamtramck City Hall.

This unassuming shoe repair shop at Caniff Avenue and Mitchell Street was demolished in 1935 to make room for the Hamtramck Post Office, which was built at a cost of $79,000. The new building was dedicated in May 1936 and is a fine example of art deco architecture. The building is still decorated with three murals by Schomer Lichtner, done as a Works Progress Administration project and installed in 1940.

Most people today know Gallagher Street as a main thoroughfare, but until 1942, the street ended before crossing Caniff Avenue. In that year, the intervening houses were removed, and the street was extended. It signified two factors: Hamtramck was continuing to grow and needed to accommodate more traffic, and that even during World War II, some large municipal projects were completed. The grand opening of the street was a major event. Several of the homes from the time are still standing.

Gallagher Street north of Caniff Avenue has changed little in the last 50 years. Unlike much of the rest of Hamtramck, this street boasts some of the finest brick houses in the city. They were quite different from the early immigrant wood-frame houses and the multifamily houses that remain much more typical. Many of the original trees, however, were wiped out by Dutch elm disease in the late 1950s and early 1960s.

White Eagle Laundry was well known in Hamtramck for many years, but ultimately it was done in by its location at 2925 Evaline Street, just off of Jos. Campau. It was demolished in the early 1950s to make room for a municipal parking lot to help alleviate the parking situation, which became acute after World War II as more residents acquired cars. Below, the three men in the first row are, from left to right, Edward, Henry, and Walter Kopek. The trio owned the laundry, which was founded by their father, George Kopek, in 1915. The parking lot is still in use. (Below, photograph courtesy of Henry S. Kopek Jr.)

The walls rise at the Colonel Hamtramck housing project on the far northwest side of the city in early 1942. Designed for 300 families, the development almost immediately became embroiled in controversy when the city attempted to refuse to allow African Americans to live in the facility. That resulted in a protracted court case, which was finally settled in 1954, when the courts ruled the project should be integrated. Over the years, it has been modernized several times and remains in use.

The construction of the viaduct on Conant Avenue south of Holbrook Avenue in 1935 eased a serious traffic problem caused by trains that crossed Conant. But no one expected the viaduct approaches below ground level to turn into a lake whenever it rained. While children enjoyed the makeshift swimming hole, it posed a serious health and safety danger. The problem was solved in the 1950s with the installation of a huge storm drain under Conant. The road has been dry ever since.

Hamtramck's police department became a real force in 1916 when four officers were hired by Chief Barney Whalen, who had been the village's sole officer up to that time. It grew rapidly thereafter. In 1941, the police took ownership of a new line of squad cars. Receiving them in the vintage photograph are, from left to right, Sgt. John Kowalski, Charles May, Joseph Trojnarski, and Jim Yergensen. Today the cars have changed substantially, but Chief Marek Kalinowski has the same task of keeping the peace in town.

The Hamtramck Fire Department took possession of a new Seagrave ladder truck in 1956 at the fire station at Mackay and Caniff Avenues. Because of the number of factories in the early days of the city and the tall two-family houses, the city has always needed equipment capable of reaching high places and delivering a large amount of firefighting power. That remains true today, as the firefighters use an updated ladder truck.

Caniff Avenue near Lumpkin Street has changed greatly in some ways and little in others since the early 1950s. Several of the buildings remain, but the Gulf gas station (at center) is long gone, replaced by a store. Interestingly, the telephone booth at the corner, which was there for decades, served as the set for a key scene in the movie *Scarecrow* starring Al Pacino and Gene Hackman in 1973.

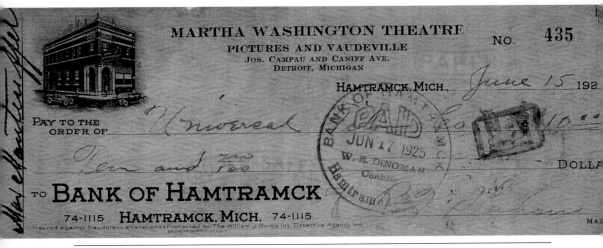

The Bank of Hamtramck was founded on November 24, 1923, and was the city's 19th bank. The image of its original front on Mitchell and Caniff Avenues is shown on a 1929 check drawn on the bank by another Hamtramck landmark, Martha Washington Theatre. The bank changed its name to Bank of Commerce in 1946 and moved a block over to Jos. Camau and Caniff Avenues, where it eventually became National City Bank. The corner doorway was filled in, but the building remains.

Liberty State Bank originally occupied the building at the corner of Jos. Campau and Norwalk Avenues. It was owned by Joseph Chronowski, who emblazoned his initials in stone at the top of the building, where they remain visible today. The bank soon moved down the street, and the building is now occupied by the Polish Art Center. Freedman Bros. Jewelers is long gone.

When Edmund Tyszka came to Hamtramck, lots on Jos. Campau Avenue sold for $400. By 1920, when he operated the Tyszka Savings Bank and the real estate agency next door, Jos. Campau lots were selling for $25,000. His business was so successful he branched out to Detroit in 1950. Tyszka died in 1975 at age 83. The building still stands but with a far different use—it houses a Hungry Howie's and a Chicken Shack.

Upon the death of his parents in 1929, at just 16 years of age Alois Grzecki took over the operations of the Florian Greenhouse—the largest in Hamtramck at the time. Located at the corner of Florian and Bromach Streets, it was well situated just across the street from St. Florian School and the adjoining church, which was also the largest in Hamtramck. The Grzecki family remained prominent in Hamtramck for decades. Alois's son Joseph Grzecki served as mayor, and his grandson, Joseph Grzecki Jr., was city treasurer. The greenhouse is gone, but the attached buildings are still standing.

Holbrook Avenue just east of Brombach Street gets a new layer of asphalt around 1960. To the right is the Orlikowski funeral home, which was an institution in Hamtramck for decades and which still stands. The left side of the street has undergone a complete transformation and is now the site of the Hamtramck Senior Plaza housing complex and the Hamtramck Town Center shopping mall.

Café 1923 at Holbrook and Dubois Streets is one of the most colorful buildings in Hamtramck. Opened as a butcher shop and grocery store in 1923 by Bernice and Paul Zukowski, the store closed decades ago and stood empty and decaying. But in 2006, new owners Sean Kowalski, his wife, Armen Gulian, and Shannon Lowell renovated and restored the store, retaining many of the original details. Sean is the great-grandson of the Zukowskis. His grandparents Harriett and John Poplawski also ran the store, keeping it in the family for four generations. Today Café 1923 is a popular coffee shop that has become a focal point of the city's social scene.

Roosevelt Street at Gallagher Street has changed little since the vintage photograph was taken around 1960. Notable here is the home with the ornate Ionic columns, an unusual design for working class Hamtramck. The ubiquitous corner store was a typical sight. There were hundreds of these stores around Hamtramck that flourished in the days before mega-supermarkets and shopping malls. They made shopping convenient and were affordable, especially for little things like candy, which sold at three pieces for a penny.

LEARNING

A group of students works in an art class in the 1930s. Hamtramck's public school system was among the finest in the nation, starting with the 1927 school code spearheaded by superintendent Maurice Keyworth. He introduced innovative concepts, such as health and dental clinics inside the schools, cutting edge technology such as a high school radio station, and critically important bilingual education classes.

The Hamtramck public school system developed slowly in the 19th century when Hamtramck Township was a rural community. Most of the early school buildings are long gone. But Holbrook Elementary School, which was opened in 1896, has survived the years and remains in use today. Once a four-story building, the top floor burned in the late 1920s and was not rebuilt. But the rest of the building, including the quaint fireplaces, remains (although the fireplaces are not used anymore).

In response to the growing population, Hamtramck High School was opened in September 1915, with grades six through nine. A grade was added each year thereafter until a full complement of courses was provided. A west wing was built in 1916 and an east wing in 1917, followed by a vocational school in 1924. The first graduating class in June 1919 had nine members. But by the late 1960s, the building was crumbling and enrollment was declining. It was closed in 1971 and demolished in 1973. Today the site is occupied by the Henry Ford Medical Center.

Hamtramck High School, Hamtramck, Mich.

Copernicus Junior High School opened in September 1931 with 2,270 pupils enrolled in grades seven, eight, and nine. It was developed to accommodate the exploding student population of Hamtramck, as the city's overall population reached 56,000 people. Recognizing that the overwhelming number of students were of Polish background, school superintendent Maurice Keyworth began a practice of naming school buildings for Polish national heroes. Today the school operates as Hamtramck High School.

When it was built in 1931, Copernicus Junior High School on Charest and Casmere Streets was considered one of the most modern in the nation. Among its special features was an operating radio station with a professional broadcasting booth. When Hamtramck High School closed and was demolished in the early 1970s, Copernicus was converted into the high school. The radio station is silent, but the other areas of the school, like the ornate library, remain virtually unchanged.

The first band class at Copernicus Junior High School practices outside the school on June 16, 1932. The school still has a band, but the practice site has long been converted into a parking lot. Other than a new roof added a few years ago, little has changed on the exterior of the building.

Pulaski School was originally named Whitney School when it was built in 1917 on the old Whitney farm on Lumpkin at Edwin Streets. Reflecting the influx of Polish immigrants, the school was named Pulaski School in honor of Casimer Pulaski, a hero of Poland. Through the years, students took part in parades to mark the opening of the recreation department's season of activities. The school closed in 1967 and was demolished soon afterward. The site was converted into a park where children play and movies are now shown during the summer.

St. Florian School opened in 1909 as a combination church and school building. By 1922, a separate church building had been constructed next door, and the original building was expanded and converted solely into a school. The immigrant population that flooded into Hamtramck after 1910 was made up primarily of Polish Catholics, and the old school building held an astounding 2,853 students by 1924. The high school closed in 2002, and the grade school closed three years later. Today the building plays host to the Frontier International Academy, a charter school.

St. Florian School and Church, Hamtramck, Mich.

The St. Florian Education Center was built in 1952 to expand athletic and class space, and to compete with what was offered to students in the public schools. Shortly after it was completed, it burned but was quickly rebuilt at its site on Poland Street, just across from St. Florian School. The center capped a building program initiated by pastor Peter P. Walkowiak. It included a large gymnasium, laboratory, classrooms, and space for the school radio station, K8LEY. After the St. Florian high school and grade school closed, the education center found new life as the Hanley International Academy charter school.

The cornerstone of Immaculate Conception Ukrainian Catholic Elementary School was laid on June 10, 1950, just next to the church on McDougall Street, which had been built 10 years earlier. Eventually a high school would be opened on Hanley Street, but both schools later closed. The building now serves as the Early Childhood Education School for the Hamtramck Public School District, but it has changed little over the years.

CHAPTER

SIGNS OF FAITH

Our Lady Queen of Apostles Church was founded in 1917, but the present impressive church building on Conant Avenue was dedicated in 1950. The church was created when St. Florian Parish, just to the southwest, grew so quickly it could not accommodate the number of parishioners.

The Polish immigrants brought a deep faith in the Catholic religion with them when they came to Hamtramck. This was shown in the many ceremonies, events, and parades conducted by the churches in town.

St. Florian Parish was the first parish in the city, having been established in 1907. The neighborhood grew up around it as Polish immigrants moved into the area. It was said that no Pole would build a house unless he could see a church steeple through the window. St. Florian seemed to prove that.

Today the neighborhood around the parish still reflects its earlier days, although all houses have been modernized. It is recognized as a National Historic District for representing a traditional immigrant community.

Although St. Florian was the first and largest parish in the city, for decades the Felician nuns who taught at the parish school and served the church were lodged in two houses across the street, rather than in a convent. In the 1950s, when the number of nuns grew to 30, the time had come for a real convent to be built. In 1958, the new convent was dedicated on Florian Street across from the school. After the schools closed, the Felicians left, and the convent is currently used for Polish language classes, meetings, and housing for some new immigrants.

Ukrainian Catholic Church   Українська Католицька Церква
Hamtramck, Michigan

While Poles came to dominate Hamtramck with their sheer numbers, they were not the only ethnic group in the town. Immaculate Conception Ukrainian Catholic Parish was established in 1913 in a modest wooden building on Grayling Street. In 1941, construction began on an impressive Byzantine edifice on Casmere Street, just beating the shortages caused by World War II. The Ukrainian faithful still worship there.

For decades, the Sunoco fuel tanks were a landmark on Holbrook Avenue east of Conant Avenue. They formed one of two concentrations of fuel tanks in the city; the other still stands at the far northwest corner of the city. The Holbrook tanks and the surrounding yard, however, were demolished in 1996. The scene is now dominated by the Kingdom Hall of Jehovah's Witnesses.

On September 19, 1987, Pope John Paul II visited Hamtramck to deliver his message on a massive stage on Jos. Campau Avenue near Holbrook Avenue. The Polish pope had strong connections to Hamtramck, including a family tie; his cousin was a city councilman in the 1940s and 1950s. Today the Hamtramck Town Center shopping mall occupies the site of the pope's stage. A monument featuring a miniature re-creation of the stage marks the occasion and location.

CHAPTER 4

SHOPPING

JOS. CAMPAU

The Tyszka Real Estate Company was one of the earliest businesses on Jos. Campau Avenue and helped build the street into one of the finest shopping districts in the state. Since the beginning of the 20th century, Jos. Campau Avenue has been the commercial lifeline of the city, running directly down its length. It was known for its high-quality products and first-rate service. Edward and Helen Tyszka are pictured behind the counter in the historical photograph.

Although Hamtramck was known as Dodge City because of its association with the Dodge Brothers factory, other manufacturers offered their iron along the strip of Jos. Campau north of Caniff Avenue known as Automobile Row. The new Ford V-8 model was introduced at Northeastern Motors Sales, which was located on this strip. The site today is incorporated into the parking lot of the popular Clock restaurant. Zena Ziekinski takes ownership of a new Ford in the vintage photograph.

Beginning in 1910, the north end of Jos. Campau was dominated for decades by auto dealers, dealer suppliers, and services such as car washes and mechanics. Dodges dominated, but Pontiacs and Chevrolets could be purchased there. Even Vauxhall, a British car company and one-time subsidiary of General Motors, could be found on Jos. Campau.

Krajenke Buick was one of the most venerable dealerships along Jos. Campau. Founder Stanley F. Krajenke was the first person to own an automobile in Hamtramck. His dealership grew out of a garage he founded in 1913. He originally sold Hupmobiles but switched to Buicks in 1922, and his dealership grew to be the largest Buick outlet in the world by the 1950s. The dealerships are gone, giving way to new businesses, like Maine Street restaurant.

Greater prosperity led to more cars—and traffic. North of Caniff Avenue, the city installed safety zones where pedestrians could take cover from the stream of traffic. Too often, however, these safety zones were anything but safe, with cars regularly plowing into them. Finally the city removed them in 1952, with no apparent affect on safety or traffic.

Johnny Motor Sales, located at 11620 Jos. Campau, was a typical auto dealership, offering a full range of Plymouths for sale. Johnny Motor Sales was part of the Hamtramck Auto Dealers' Association, which included Edmund Olds, Krajenke Buick, Woody Pontiac, and Connell Cadillac (later Chevrolet). Competitors yet associates, they formed a powerful business bloc that gave northern Hamtramck an identity as the place to go to buy a new car. The site is now occupied by a Little Caesars restaurant.

Pieronek Studios photographed Hamtramck for more than 70 years, chronicling legions of first communions, weddings, city officials, places, and events. Paul Pieronek moved his studio, originally located on Chene Street in Detroit, to Hamtramck on Jos. Campau between Whalen and Pulaski Streets in 1923. The business closed in 2002, and the building was eventually donated to the Piast Institute, an organization for Polish affairs. A new facade has modernized the building.

This series of photographs shows the evolution of a site, part of the natural changing life of a city. Woody Pontiac was founded in 1940 by Woodrow W. Woody and grew to become the largest Pontiac dealership in the nation. Over the years, the dealership on Jos. Campau changed physically, expanding and acquiring a new facade. In 2000, at the age of 92, Woody retired from the business, and the landmark dealership closed.

The Woody Pontiac dealership building stood vacant and began to deteriorate after it closed in 2000. But the site acquired new life in 2009 when the State of Michigan announced plans to build a new department of human services office there. The old dealership was demolished, the site was cleared, and construction began on a 30,000-square-foot, $8.5 million new building to be called Woody Plaza. From life to death to life again, the site has gone full circle.

Like most car dealerships, Woody Pontiac offered a variety of used as well as new cars. In 1942, Woody's lot was across the street from his dealership on Jos. Campau Avenue at the north end of town, next to the Nite Own Inn, one of the city's popular watering holes. Today the Nite Owl has vanished, although cars still occupy a lot on the site of Woody's old dealership annex.

The Nite Owl Inn on Jos. Campau Avenue was typical of the hundreds of bars in Hamtramck in the 1940s. "Dance to the Music That Makes You Dance," proclaimed its advertisement in the *Hamtramck Citizen* newspaper on December 12, 1942. John S. Cieslak provided the music with his accordion. Offering choice liquors, wines, and beers, the Nite Owl proclaimed, "You'll find the atmosphere most congenial, the drinks perfect, and the most popular prices prevail." Today the site is occupied by a rather utilitarian business building.

A host of Hamtramck landmarks clustered at the intersection of Jos. Campau and Caniff Avenues in 1957. At the southeast corner stood Cunningham's Drugs, the counterpart of another Cunningham's Drugs a quarter-mile farther south at Holbrook and Jos. Campau Avenues. Just south of the north Cunningham's was Lendzon's department store and still farther south was Max's Jewelry. On the southwest corner of the intersection was Martha Washington Theatre, one of seven movie houses in the city. Although Martha Washington Theatre was demolished in the early 1990s and the other businesses are closed, the buildings remain.

Jos. Campau and Caniff Avenues glowed with lights at night during Christmas in 1955. Jos. Campau was at its peak in the 1950s and was one of the most popular shopping districts in the state of Michigan. Nearly every type of business was represented here, with the Good Housekeeping shop a particular favorite. Businesses still thrive on Jos. Campau, although most of the old stores have long since gone.

Max's Jewelry was one of the most beloved businesses in Hamtramck's history. Owner Max Rosenbaum founded the business in 1913 in Detroit. A few years later, he opened a store at Goodson Street and Jos. Campau Avenue, and in 1934, the store was moved to Jos. Campau near Holbrook Avenue. In 1940, Max's Jewelry opened at the location most people remember. It survived fires and changing times but eventually closed in the 1980s. The building is in use today as another jewelry outlet, Gold and Glitter Jewelry.

The heart of Jos. Campau at Belmont Street in 1955 was a busy place and remains so today. At the southeast corner stood Peter C. Jezewski's Apteka—Polish for pharmacy. It was notable for its sale of live leeches. Jezewski was Hamtramck's first mayor, and his pharmacy was also his political headquarters. The southwest corner of the intersection is now the site of Pope Park, honoring Pope John Paul II.

In the early 1960s, Jos. Campau Avenue still had not been affected much by the growth of suburban shopping malls. Day's Fashions, at right, was typical of the women's clothing stores that were especially popular along the strip. The Pol Art Center, at left center, now is known as the Polish Art Center and remains a popular and internationally known business that has been featured on the Cooking Channel and Travel Channel for its unique imported goods.

Even in the depths of World War II, some luxury items could be found for sale. Atlas 5th Avenue Fashions featured a line of fine furs displayed prominently in the front windows. There is no record of when the store at 10020 Jos. Campau Avenue closed, but the building is still in use. It has played host to the Urban Break coffee house and, most recently, has operated as the Pro Nails salon.

The Warsaw Bakery was one of the numerous bakeries that were—and still are—a key component of the Jos. Campau shopping district. Like most of the buildings on Jos. Campau Avenue, it has been extensively remodeled. Many of the buildings have been totally gutted and rebuilt. When this building was remodeled, however, care was taken by the owner to preserve the distinctive decorative stonework above the door, which is visible in the vintage and modern photographs.

Jos. Campau Avenue at the intersection of Poland Street in 1941 played host to Dave Stober clothes, one of Hamtramck's legendary stores. Stober later moved to new quarters farther up Jos. Campau and remained in business until the 1970s. His store, flanked by more fashion stores, helped cement Jos. Campau's image as the place to shop for fine clothes. The building has been occupied by several businesses since then.

Pure Food grocery store opened at 9715 Jos. Campau Avenue in 1933, but moved to a bigger building at 9325 Jos. Campau Avenue in 1939. In 1943, a second store was opened at 9727 Jos. Campau Avenue. Interestingly, both stores were identical to each other except they faced in opposite direction, making them mirror copies. In 1961, the stores hid their old faces as their facades were covered with modern siding. No longer grocery stores, both buildings remain in use and still retain their curious mirror images.

Hamtramck's First Drive-in Banking Facility—Liberty State Bank

Liberty State Bank opened in 1918 with $100,000 in capital. Two years later, the bank moved to an impressive Greek Revival structure two blocks south at the corner of Jos. Campau and Holbrook Avenues. It was one of the few banks in town to survive the Great Depression. Liberty State Bank adapted to the times by adding drive-though windows in 1964, but the original structure remains nearly unchanged. The bank is now part of the Huntington Bank company.

The Jos. Campau–Holbrook Building was one of the most beautiful—and controversial—structures in Hamtramck. Construction of the building began in 1928 but remained incomplete for more than a decade, a victim of the Great Depression. It was labeled an eyesore, and the building's owner and the city battled over its appearance in court before it was finally finished in the late 1930s. It housed a variety of offices and finally a Big Boy restaurant until 1992, when it burned, and the remains were demolished.

The intersection of Jos. Campau and Holbrook Avenues was one of the key crossroads of early Hamtramck. Until 1905, a creek ran along Holbrook in a ravine nearly 20 feet deep. This was filled in and replaced by Holbrook Avenue, which became a principal cross street. Peoples State Bank, established in 1909, originally stood on the southwest corner (at the right). It later moved to the opposite corner, where it remains today. This view looks south, toward Detroit. The Baker Street Car line ran down Jos. Campau and connected Hamtramck to downtown Detroit.

Joseph Campau Ave. from Holbrook, Hamtramck, Mich.

The decorative clock on Peoples State Bank at the corner of Jos. Campau and Holbrook Avenues was a familiar landmark for years. The bank, the oldest in Hamtramck, was modernized with a new facade in the 1960s. Cunningham's was a popular drugstore known especially for its long soda fountain bar at the back. The site is occupied by a CVS drugstore today, and the intersection remains one of the busiest in the city.

MARGOLIS FURNITURE CO.
9130 Jos. Campau, Detroit 12, Michigan. TR-inity 1-15
Branch 5560 Chene Street. WA-lnut 1-9756

Margolis furniture, at 9130 Jos. Campau Avenue, was one of several furniture stores on Jos. Campau, and likely the largest. It offered a variety of high quality furniture. A few blocks from the modern showroom stood Margolis's warehouses, just off Jos. Campau at Wyandotte Street. In the 1980s, the store was demolished and replaced with a McDonald's fast food restaurant, which continues to serve burgers in the same location.

Below Holbrook stands the South End, the oldest area of Hamtramck. The city developed from the south to the north along Jos. Campau Avenue, mainly after 1910. In the vintage photograph, workers clean snow off the corner of Goodson Street and Jos. Campau Avenue in 1957. At the left in the vintage photograph is the old Playdium bowling alley, and just to the right of the furniture store is what had been a social hall for years. Recently, the building was converted into fine lofts.

ZT Supermarket was typical of the local stores that thrived before the development of the large chain grocery stores. The store, operated by Z. Tomaszewski and Theodore Pypkowski, featured dressed poultry, fresh fruits, vegetables, and canned foods, along with highest-grade meats. The site is now occupied by the drive-through of the McDonald's restaurant.

A parade, likely on Memorial Day 1946, gives an insight into the streetscape. Barely visible at the upper right in the vintage photograph is the White Tower hamburger restaurant. That places the scene at Jos. Campau Avenue and Geimer Street, with the officers marching south along the Baker Street Car line. Also of note is Skurski Quality Shoes. The site today makes up part of the parking lot of the Hamtramck Town Center shopping mall.

The Jewell Theater and an early post office branch occupied the joint building constructed in 1912 and 1913 on Jos. Campau Avenue, just north of the viaduct. Through the years, many businesses have occupied the buildings, which are among the oldest extant in the city. Today upscale apartments fill the upper floor. The Jewell Theater was one of the earliest in the Hamtramck area. Local resident Terry Paris seems to step out of time to take a place in the contemporary photograph.

The Dodge Main overpass can just be seen at the far left of the vintage photograph dating from 1954. Equally prominent at the time were the twin gas tanks in the distance at left. These elements, together with the smokestacks at right, epitomized industrial Hamtramck at its peak. All these symbols are gone today but not what they represented. This entire area is now within the bounds of the General Motors Detroit-Hamtramck Assembly Plant. Two modern tanks now stand roughly where the old tanks stood.

SHOPPING JOS. CAMPAU

GOOD TIMES

A. Buhr's bar was typical of what would be found in Hamtramck just prior to the influx of the immigrant population that began in 1910. At that time, most residents of the village of Hamtramck were of German descent. (Bar patrons were known then as "stammgasts.") From the earliest days, bars were the social centers of the town. In the years after Prohibition, there were hundreds operating in Hamtramck, which then had more bars per capita than any city in America. Hamtramckans, however, found many more socially acceptable ways of having fun through the years.

Leo Rau was one of the more colorful characters in Hamtramck. His House of Rau bar was filled to the rafters—literally—with odd items like buckets and steer horns. Its proprietor fostered an equally odd image. Rau sported a goatee and top hat in the 1940s, when such adornments were not usual. The House of Rau existed at two places, 11414 Jos. Campau Avenue and 2921 Trowbridge Street. The Campau site is now a restaurant parking lot, and the Trowbridge site was most recently a soup restaurant.

The Farnum Theater was one of seven movie houses that existed in Hamtramck over the years. The Farnum opened in 1918 with 900 seats and lasted until 1967, when it was demolished. Its site across from Wyandotte Street at 9048 Jos. Campau Avenue has variously been occupied by a credit union, Chinese restaurant, and, most recently, a Family Dollar store. Like the other movie houses, Farnum showed second- and third-run features and occasionally hosted live shows. Some of the theaters also showed Polish-language films.

The Conant Theater was built in 1929 with 940 seats. However, it could not withstand the onslaught of television and was one of the victims of a dwindling audience drawn away by the tiny TV sets. It closed in 1954 and stood vacant for decades. The site was finally cleared and the land reused for a strip mall. Although the building is gone, a few of its glazed white bricks have been saved.

The Playdium bowling alley on Jos. Campau Avenue outlasted the city's other bowling alley, Northend Recreation at the other end of Jos. Campau. For decades the Playdium was the home of the Citizen Bowling Classic, which drew thousands of bowlers each year to take part in the high-stakes tournament. After the Playdium closed, the building was demolished, and a Checkers hamburger stand occupies this site. But Playdium is hardly forgotten, as collectors have saved some of the prized bowling pins.

Veterans Memorial Park is by far the largest park in Hamtramck. Since 1962, it has been the final resting place of Col. John Francis Hamtramck, the city's eponymous founder. The war memorial is inscribed with the names of all Hamtramckans who have died in the nation's wars. One of two state historical markers in the park honors Colonel Hamtramck. The other notes the history of the Dodge Brothers, who built the Dodge Main factory and were responsible for the development of modern Hamtramck.

Youngsters play on the teeter-totter at Veterans Memorial Park. Once a swamp, then a lumber yard, the park evolved over the years to include tennis courts and playground equipment. It was here that Jean Hoxie trained her world champion tennis teams and where the 1959 Little League and 1961 Pony League world champion teams played. The old playground equipment has been replaced in recent years, and children continue to have fun.

The 8,000-seat Keyworth Stadium was built in 1936 at a cost of $144,000 as a Works Progress Administration project. Unlike other WPA jobs, however, Keyworth Stadium attracted presidential attention and was dedicated by Pres. Franklin Roosevelt amid great fanfare in 1936. The stadium was built at the end of Roosevelt Street, named for the president just after his visit. Missing from the contemporary photograph is Pulaski School, which was next to the stadium (at left in the vintage photograph), but it was demolished in the 1960s.

From the 1930s to the early 1950s, the Bowery was one of the top nightclubs in the Midwest. Many top acts performed there, including Sophie Tucker, the Three Stooges, Sally Rand, and Jimmy Durante. Patrons signaled their approval of performers by tapping wooden sticks on the table tops. The Bowery was a major entertainment venue until owner Frank Barbaro and his wife, Dorothy, divorced. Barbaro's wife received ownership of the club in the divorce, and within a few years it closed. The building burned a few years after that, and now all that remains is the ghostly outline of the roofline imprinted on the wall of the building next door.

In 1923, Casimir Kocat opened C&K Brewing Company, a malt manufacturing plant in Hamtramck. He sold the business 10 years later after Prohibition ended, but the new owners retained the name. The business was initially successful, but sales soon flagged. By 1938, the brewery, which by that time had been named the Wagner Brewing Company, closed. The buildings, expanded beyond the original wooden structures, remain on Klinger Street and now are used by the Hamtramck Public Schools as a garage.

Copernicus Junior High School students plant a victory garden across the street from the north entrance of the school in June 1943. Such gardens were popular in the city as a patriotic gesture, with the bonus of being economical and fun to tend. There still was a fair amount of vacant land around the school when it was built in 1931 and during World War II, but this area was fully developed just a few years after the war.

A ball, a hoop, an open lot—those are all the elements needed to have fun now or a half-century ago. The vintage photograph dates from 1959, with the players showing their style on a lot outside of Copernicus Junior High School. The contemporary photograph shows a new generation of players in a similar court near Keyworth Stadium.

Hamtramckans have always loved parades. Memorial Day parades were popular, especially after World War II, as shown in the vintage photograph. But just about any reason was good enough to start a march down the street. Significant parades were held in 1927 to commemorate the 100th anniversary of the creation of the third Hamtramck Township, in 1937 to mark the end of the Dodge Main sit-down strike, and in 1945 to celebrate the end of World War II. In recent years, Paczki Day, a Polish celebration held the day before Lent begins, has proven to be a popular reason for a colorful parade and loads of fun.

www.arcadiapublishing.com

Discover books about the town where you grew up, the cities where your friends and families live, the town where your parents met, or even that retirement spot you've been dreaming about. Our Web site provides history lovers with exclusive deals, advanced notification about new titles, e-mail alerts of author events, and much more.

MADE IN THE USA

Arcadia Publishing, the leading local history publisher in the United States, is committed to making history accessible and meaningful through publishing books that celebrate and preserve the heritage of America's people and places. Consistent with our mission to preserve history on a local level, this book was printed in South Carolina on American-made paper and manufactured entirely in the United States.

This book carries the accredited Forest Stewardship Council (FSC) label and is printed on 100 percent FSC-certified paper. Products carrying the FSC label are independently certified to assure consumers that they come from forests that are managed to meet the social, economic, and ecological needs of present and future generations.

FSC
Mixed Sources
Product group from well-managed
forests and other controlled sources

Cert no. SW-COC-001530
www.fsc.org
© 1996 Forest Stewardship Council

Find Your Place in History.